FLUTE SOLO

from

SCARAMOUCHE

Op. 71

Jean Sibelius

FLØJTESOLO
Tranquillo assai

dolce ed espressivo

meno dolce

dolce

meno dolce

dim.

WILHELM HANSEN EDITION NO. 4220

JEAN SIBELIUS

FLUTE SOLO

from

SCARAMOUCHE

Op. 71

Arranged for flute and piano

by Jussi Jalas

Edition Wilhelm Hansen A/S, Copenhagen
Edition Wilhelm Hansen / Chester Music New York Inc.
Distribution: Magnamusic-Baton Inc.
J. og W. Chester / Edition Wilhelm Hansen London Ltd.
Edition Wilhelm Hansen Frankfurt a. M.
AB Nordiska Musikförlaget / Edition Wilhelm Hansen Stockholm
Norsk Musikforlag A/S Oslo

FLUTE SOLO

from

SCARAMOUCHE

Op. 71

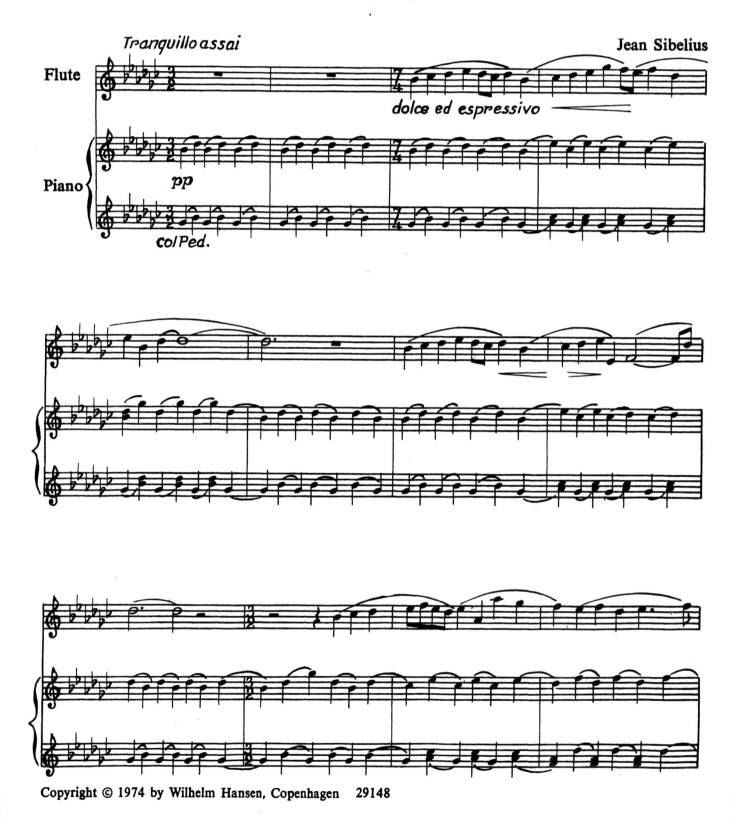

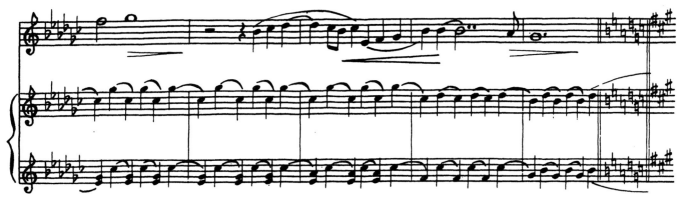

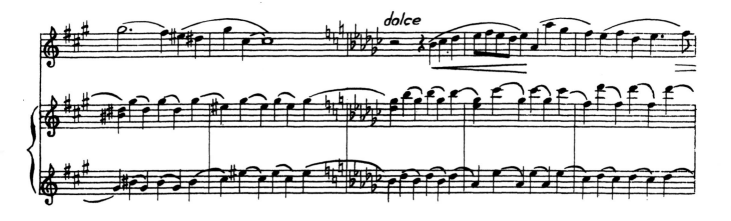

4

meno dolce

dim.

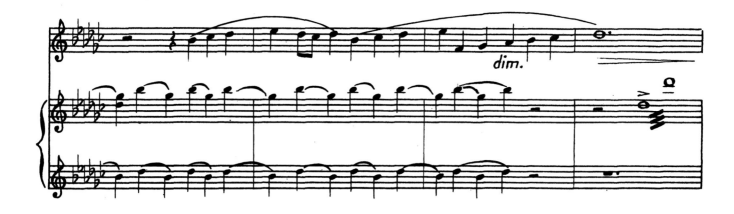

sf